What readers are saying

"It was definitely an 'A-HA' experience in reading about these concepts in *Out of the Red*...I could see how they applied to my business."

"If you love making money, but don't understand the financial details... *Out of the Red* is for you."

"These are such critical concepts. How come no one mentioned them to me before?"

OUT OF THE RED
© 2005

Pam Newman
RPPC, Inc.
www.rppc.net

Published by Small Business Resource
Missouri

To order the book:

Phone: 816.304.4398
Toll-free: 1.866.206.0824
E-mail: rppc@rppc.net

Published by Small Business Resource

Copyright © 2005 by Pam Newman

Edited by Ingrid L. Abraham-Turner

Cover design by Trinity3 Marketing & Advertising

This publication is designed to provide accurate and authoritative information in regard to the subject matter covered. It is sold with the understanding that the publisher and author are providing information and not specific consultation to your business. The services of a competent professional management accountant should be sought to help you apply this information as needed for your specific situation.

ISBN: 0-9764408-0-6

This book is dedicated to all the small business owners who make our country the success it is today. Small businesses are the sign of opportunity in our world. It is part of the American Dream…that anyone can have the chance to be a business owner. I've been blessed to have the opportunity to be an entrepreneur through various businesses with my husband. Those entrepreneurial opportunities have made a larger impact in my life than my corporate experiences and education combined. It's truly "on the job" experience that cannot be explained to those who've not felt the extreme highs and lows of running their own business. I wouldn't exchange my experiences for anything in the world. When you feel unsure…it is those times that you know you are blazing a new path!

Our family's motto is "Wish it…Dream it…Do it". There are wishers, dreamers and doers. Which will you be? This book is written to help the doers in achieving success in their business. These concepts we'll explore are critical parts to the overall success of business and I wish you well on your journey!

Thank you to my family, friends, and clients. You have provided me the opportunity to lead the life I've always dreamed of!

INTRODUCTION

This book is written to introduce you to Management Accounting concepts that you, as a small business owner, should be utilizing in your management decision-making process. Some of the concepts we'll cover include Break-even Point Analysis, Gross Profit Margin Ratio, Net Profit Margin Ratio, Profit/Loss Statement, Balance Sheet, Cash Flow, Budgeting, Current Ratio, and Return on Assets—just to name a few.

The purpose of this book is to introduce you to the most critical Management Accounting concepts and peak your interest to learn more about them. While it could have been a 'how to' book, I felt that it would better serve your needs by giving you a general financial overview so you could partner with a Management Accountant to learn how these concepts apply to your business. These concepts can seem overwhelming, but teaming up with a good small business professional will aid you in your understanding. The stories throughout this book will highlight how various types of small businesses have utilized these different concepts in the success of their business. Once you have completed reading this book, I encourage you to create an action plan on how you will follow-up on this book by asking yourself these questions: How will you start learning more about these concepts? How can they add value to your business and keep you 'out of the red'?

Today, as entrepreneurs, we are bombarded with having to wear so many hats that it can be very overwhelming. Instead of facing the issues that deal with our businesses, some small business owners try to hide from the facts. Others are too wrapped up in the day-to-day running of their business that they unknowingly fail to realize the importance of utilizing the accounting information in their decision-making process.

By accounting information, I'm not referring to taxes. Instead I'll be focusing on the management aspects of accounting and how you can utilize your financial statements to help you make better business decisions. This information can help you find answers to questions such as: How do I set my prices? How do I determine how many products or hours of service I need to provide to cover my fixed costs? How much can I afford to pay for an employee?

Financial responsibility can be one of the scariest aspects of starting and operating a small business because there are so many things to know. Looking at all those numbers on a page can easily overwhelm anyone! Why do you think so many businesses fail? The unfortunate answer is that the owners simply 'don't know what they don't know.' This book is designed to help introduce you to various aspects of Management Accounting and how it can contribute to the success of your business. But keep in mind a word of caution; this book isn't designed to teach you how to be an Accountant. Instead, it was written to make you aware of some of the lingo, concepts and successes other business owners similar to you have had that have kept them in business.

Most small businesses fail because they aren't able to operate profitably. Most failures could have been prevented through accurate analysis of their financial statements and utilization of that information into their business decision-making model. There are warning signs when a business is not doing well, but we aren't always receptive to them so we look the other way and think it will get better on its own. But we can't be passive in running our businesses. There are many factors that we are up against as small business owners. We can't afford to sit back and see where we end up. We need to be proactive by taking control of that steering wheel to ensure we take the right path!

Think about the most successful outcomes in your life. Did they happen during the easiest times? NO! When we look at our successes, we normally see them falling on the timeline of our lives after the most difficult times. Running a business isn't any different. It takes a lot of hard work to make sure all the aspects are covered. As a business owner, we have to think about operations, customers, vendors, bankers, government regulations, tax collectors, accounting, strategic planning, and a whole lot more.

There is never 'enough' time. You can't ignore all the demands a business makes on you, but you do have to prioritize everything that needs to be done. You have to decide which areas you can tackle and which areas you need to surround yourself with others who have complimentary skills.

Bookkeeping/Accounting usually tend to fall at the bottom of the list of skills for small business owners. As entrepreneurs, we are really good at producing our product or service, but we usually can't boast that bookkeeping is a strength. That's okay...you just have to be able to assess your strengths and weaknesses realistically and be willing to step up to the plate and ask for help. But make sure you do it sooner than later and you'll have fewer regrets because most of our regrets in life are based upon what we did NOT do versus what we did do.

Since Accounting is one of those weaknesses for a myriad of small business owners, I'm going to address the Management Accounting aspects throughout this book. There are dozens of books out there on the market covering ways to save on taxes, but what about other accounting aspects for small businesses? Quality management of a business HAS to incorporate

7

Management Accounting because it is like the flour in your cake recipe...your business recipe won't turn out the same if you don't include the key ingredients!

Note for clarification: I will mention the concepts of Bookkeeping and Management Accounting often throughout this book. These are two different points on the Accounting continuum. Bookkeeping is a part of Management Accounting and Management Accounting incorporates the larger picture of bookkeeping, financial statement preparation, analysis, budgeting, and other financial concepts.

I hope you'll enjoy the stories of small business owners just like yourself, who benefited from incorporating these simple steps into the management of their business. Now, let's share in their successes and make them yours! (The names and locations have been changed to protect the identities of the business owners.)

MEET OUR SMALL BUSINESS OWNERS

Dean

- ☐ Owns a trucking company in the middle of Iowa.
- ☐ Has been in business about eleven years.
- ☐ What is the difference between cash flow and profit?

Paige

- ☐ New entrepreneur in her mid-twenties.
- ☐ Daycare business.
- ☐ What is her Break-even point?

Cole

- ☐ Roofer in Kansas.
- ☐ Doesn't have a knack for the 'numbers part'.
- ☐ What's important to know?

Cristi

- She is in her mid-thirties.
- She has been in business about four years in Missouri.
- Promotional advertisement business.
- Looking to move out of her basement and into a storefront on the main street in her town.
- What kind of analysis needs to be considered prior to this move?

Dawn and Cody

- Both are in their late 50's.
- They own an orchard and pumpkin farm in Western Iowa.
- Are they charging more than the market can handle?

Patty and Jan

- ☐ They live in Northern Illinois.
- ☐ Patty's background is in Marketing and Jan's is in Computer Technology.
- ☐ What questions should they be asking themselves each month?

Donna

- ☐ In her late 60's.
- ☐ Starting a consulting company in Colorado.
- ☐ Needs someone to help her with some of the basic administrative issues.
- ☐ What is the best option for her?

Kate

- ☐ In her mid-forties.
- ☐ Lives in Western Kansas.
- ☐ How can she bring people in the door without spending all of her profits on advertising?

Staci

- ☐ Owner of a new salon in Southern Missouri.
- ☐ Sales are difficult to project.
- ☐ Why is a budget so important for her to have?

All of these business owners have something in common...they need the help of a Management Accountant to help them learn about the 'numbers' aspect of their business and how to run their business more effectively through proactive management of their financials. There are so many aspects to consider. How do we know what to look for and where to find the answers? How do we keep our business 'out of the red'? These are just two of the numerous questions that every small business owner should ask him or herself as they make steps to take their business to the next level.

Most small business owners seek out assistance from tax professionals, but what about the management aspects? Why don't people spend time educating themselves on how they can use the numbers to aid in business management? Most of the time it is a case of 'not knowing what they don't know.'

Throughout life we hear a lot about taxes and how much we have to pay whether we are an employee or a business owner. Society focuses a lot on taxes so we are familiar with those aspects of running a business. At least we know we've got to find someone to help us address the tax issues; however, very rarely does anyone talk about the management aspects such as Profit Margin, Break-even Point, Cash Flow, Return on Assets, Budgeting, etc.

Without knowing this vital information, how can we expect our businesses to survive? An overwhelming percent of new businesses fail within the first two years based on governmental statistics. However, what about the numbers of established businesses that fail each year? It's a rare event to find a business owner who has not had at least one business idea that was not successful.

The odds are definitely against small business owners when they start, but that doesn't mean you can't overcome the obstacles you are presented with. You can learn from these examples and improve the chances of your business being successful whether you are currently thinking about going into business or have been in business for a month or a hundred years. These concepts are ones that are important to the financial success of your business. It's these concepts that separate the failures from the successes. What will be your story? Will it have a happy or a sad ending?

You'll find that although these stories may differ from yours in some ways, in other ways they will be highly symbolic of your experiences. We learn best from those who have traveled the path before us. Seize the lessons from these entrepreneurs who have been where you are today and have come out on top!

DEAN

Dean is a sole proprietor and has a trucking company in the middle of Iowa. Dean's been in business about eleven years. The first few years were great and he felt like he was making a lot of money, but he was also spending a lot!! The last few years have been a real struggle for him. The economy has been in the 'toilet' and fuel prices have skyrocketed so his margins have been minimal to negative. Dean's tried a variety of bookkeepers, tax professionals, and business consultants to keep his business on track, but nothing seems to help.

No one ever explained to Dean the difference between profit and cash flow. Previous individuals always looked at his profit/loss statement and would exclaim that he was definitely making a profit. However, no one ever showed him that 95% of that profit was going towards his principal payments on his loans.

Dean was like most of his small competitors. He had little formal education past high school and after driving a truck for a couple of years; he decided to start his own business. He was making money for his boss, so he decided to become the boss and start making the money for himself. How hard could it be? It seemed pretty clear cut to him and he'd been in the business so he was aware of the various aspects to trucking. Or at least that's what he thought....

His first few years seemed to be full of surprises. It was amazing how much money kept flowing out. The insurance, taxes, fuel, payroll, and all the other expenses kept piling up. Then his truck broke down and he ended up buying another truck instead of fixing his old one. However, business was good and the cash kept flowing in, although sometimes it was a little unsteady. As the years progressed, he added trucks to his fleet and worked his way up to having ten employees on the road and a couple in the office for dispatch and administrative assistance.

He was well aware of the hundreds of thousands of dollars that he was billing the customers and it seemed like they paid their accounts most of the time in a fairly quick manner in that the payment was usually made in 30 days or less. Dean felt that he could never build up any extra cash.

What was wrong? No one had ever mentioned that net income and cash flow were different. You can have a positive net income and still have a negative cash flow. How? There are transactions that occur in your business that do not appear on your profit and loss statement. Examples of this are the owner's withdrawals, credit card principal and loan principal payments. These activities take cash out of the business, but are not considered expenses. As the owner's withdrawal money from their business, it reduces the owner's equity in the business. Principal payments on loans and credit cards reduce the amount of the loan or credit card liability, but these payments are not considered expenses. Only the interest paid is an expense, the principal portion is not.

17

For example, if you have a net income of $5,000, but have a loan that you are paying $6,000 a month for the principal, this will create a negative cash flow of $1,000. Dean couldn't believe that no one had ever mentioned this concept to him before. Dean needed to increase his revenues and/or decrease his expenses to be able to increase his net income to cover the amount of his loan payments before he would have a positive net cash flow. This is such a simple concept when explained; however, it's one that often goes without explanation and leads businesses into a `CASH FLOW CRUNCH'.

What's a `CASH FLOW CRUNCH'? It's where you have more cash flowing out then you have flowing in and you aren't able to pay your bills or obligations. No matter how much you sell, if you don't have enough cash, then you will encounter the `CASH FLOW CRUNCH' and it has a lot to do with the timing of cash receipts and payments. Remember…CASH IS KING because it's what keeps our business going!

After explaining the difference between net profit and cash flow in further detail, Dean could easily see where his cash was going and why he felt he never had any money. Cash flow and profits are two different concepts that are both important to a business and can either make or break your business.

NOTES

PAIGE

Paige is a new entrepreneur in her mid-twenties. She established her daycare business last month in Central Nebraska. She didn't have time to develop a business plan or any of that 'nonsense'. She's been babysitting since she was a teenager, so why spend her time on all of that business stuff because she knew what to do! She couldn't find a full-time job that paid what she could make watching her friend and neighbor's kids, or so she thought.

She had a nice backyard for the kids to play in, so it seemed like the perfect business for her even though no one had ever asked her how she was going to set her prices, pay for all her added business expenses, or how many children she'd have to watch at a certain price in order to start making a profit.

In fact, Paige didn't have any business experience or anyone to help her through that process. None of her friends or family members are business owners. Little did she know that her Break-even Point, which is based on her current pricing and expenses, was going to be three kids and she only had two kids currently enrolled.

Calculating your **Break-even Point** is where you calculate how many goods or services you must sell at a given rate to cover your fixed costs to 'Break-even'. There are some costs that our businesses incur whether or not we sell any products or services and those costs are referred to as **Fixed Costs**. Fixed Costs do not change in relationship to sales activity. Some examples of fixed costs may include rent, insurance, advertising, administrative salaries, etc. **Variable Costs** are those costs that vary in relationship with sales activity. For Paige, her variable costs are groceries. She will need to calculate her **Contribution Margin** before she can proceed in calculating her **Break-even Point**. We'll assume that Paige has the following financial details broken out on a daily basis:

1. Insurance $ 10 (Fixed)
2. Licenses/Permits $ 5 (Fixed)
3. Groceries per child $ 5 (Variable)
4. Fee per day for a child $ 10 (Sales)

To calculate her **Contribution Margin**, we'll use the following formula:

Sales:	$10
Less Variable Costs:	$ 5
Equals Contribution Margin:	$ 5

The **Contribution Margin** is how much you can contribute to fixed costs from each sale. Out of each sale, you must first cover your variable costs and then your fixed costs. Then, if anything is left over, you've made a profit. To get your **Contribution Margin Ratio**, take your contribution margin in dollars and divide it by your sales dollars.

Break-even Calculation:

Fixed Costs:	$ 15
Divided by Contribution Margin	$ 5
Equals	3 Children

So what does this mean for Paige? This means that she must have a minimum number of three children per day at $10/per child just to Break-even and cover her costs. Is this okay?

Most of us don't want to just Break-even; we want to actually make a profit! If Paige has less than three children, she will be losing money each day she operates.

So what do these concepts mean to the success of Paige's business? For her, it means the difference between success and failure. Paige still has options she can consider which include increasing her daily rate per child, increasing the number of children she watches and/or decreasing her expenses. If she

24

wanted to take it to the next step and make a profit of $35 per day, she could simply change her equation to:

Calculation:

Fixed Costs plus Profit:	$50
Divided by Contribution Margin	$ 5
Equals	10 Children

This is an easy calculation that can change the path of her business. To meet her profit goal of $35 a day given the current expenses and daily childcare rate, Paige will need to have ten kids daily to achieve her goal. These simple numbers are used for reinforcing this concept.

Any business can use this equation by inputting their numbers into the equation and you'll be amazed at what you'll learn from a few simple math equations. Perhaps you've seen this equation before, but just didn't know how to interpret it or how it added value to you? It's an important concept for any business.

NOTES

COLE

Cole is a roofer in Kansas and has been roofing houses since he was old enough to climb a ladder. His dad, Rich, has had his own roofing business for 20 years. When Cole graduated from high school two years ago, he went into business with Rich. Now his dad was looking at retiring and Cole was expected to take the business over. Cole knew all the aspects of roofing as far as the manual work, how to measure and estimate for job materials, tearing the shingles off, and replacing them with new ones. What Cole didn't know a lot about was the financials. His dad had always focused on that part of the business and left the operations management to Cole. Cole didn't have a knack for the 'numbers part' and desperately needed someone to help him understand that part of his business.

Cole is like most entrepreneurs in that most of us are really good at producing the product or providing the services. That's why we went into business because we love the product or service that we provide, and not having to do all of that 'other' stuff.

(I've never heard anyone say that they went into business because they loved bookkeeping--unless that's the service they provided!) Ask any small business owner and you'll be hard-pressed to find one who says that they love doing the bookkeeping because it's usually the number one thing they hate most about being a business owner. Yet, it's at the top of the list of critical aspects to running a successful business.

Due to his lack of knowledge of the accounting aspect of running a business, Cole decided to visit some local business seminars to see what he might be able to learn about the financial management of his business. He attended a seminar entitled *"FINANCIAL STATEMENT FUNDAMENTALS"* and was able to walk away with some of the key ratios that every business owner needs to know about his/her business. While there are a million different ways to analyze your business, you don't want to get 'paralysis by analysis'. You can overanalyze your information to where the cost outweighs the benefit. It's more important to take a handful of ratios that you can use in your decision-making process and focus on them. Cole was amazed to find that the analysis of financial statements was going to be less time consuming then he had anticipated, which was a great relief to him!

The basic ratios they covered in the seminar included:

1. Net Profit Margin Ratio
2. Gross Profit Margin Ratio
3. Current Ratio
4. Return on Assets
5. Debt Ratio

Cole realized he didn't have to be a math whiz to be able to calculate and use these ratios. It is the fear of the unknown that keeps most of us from learning how to analyze our financial statements. Surely it must take years of education to learn it, right? WRONG! It's just knowing how to take the numbers off the financial statements, performing a few simple calculations and then knowing what those answers mean.

A little determination and a willingness to learn is all it takes. Cole summarized his findings with his dad, Rich, upon his return from the seminar. Rich was amazed that Cole was able to summarize what it had taken him 15+ years to acquire. Rich knew Cole would successfully take over his business and that provided him a great sense of comfort to move into the next phase of his life.

Gross Profit and Net Profit--what's the difference you might ask? To calculate your gross profit, you take your total Sales (aka revenues) and subtract out your **Cost of Goods Sold** (aka direct costs), which gives you your Gross Profit. To get to your Net Profit, take your Gross Profit and subtract your indirect costs (aka administrative & operating expenses).

The Profit/Loss Equation is:

Sales – Cost of Goods Sold = Gross Profit –
Administrative & Operating Expenses = Net Profit/Loss.

Direct costs (**Cost of Goods Sold**) include labor and
materials that are directly related to the product you
provide. Indirect costs are your administrative and
operating expenses that can include such expenses as
office supplies, advertising, rent, professional consulting
fees, interest expense, taxes, bank service charges, etc.

You can have a positive Gross Profit and end up with a
negative Net Profit. It's important that you break down
your expenses in your business into direct and indirect
so that you can analyze how you're spending your
money. To get your **Gross Profit Margin Ratio** or **Net
Profit Margin Ratio**, take your Gross Profit or Net Profit in
dollars and divide it by your Sales dollars. This
calculation provides you with a percentage.

For example, if your **Gross Profit Margin Ratio** is 25%, that means you have 25 cents out of every dollar to pay for indirect costs and still have a profit and you are spending 75 cents out of every dollar on your direct costs. **Net Profit** is the amount you have left over after all of your direct and indirect expenses are paid. If your **Net Profit Margin Ratio** is 10%, that means that out of every $1 of sales, you have 10 cents leftover after all of your direct and indirect expenses.

Remember that you have some things going on in your business that require cash but are not classified as expenses. That is why you cannot assume that Net Profit and Cash are equal. Owner's withdrawals, credit card principal payments, and loan principal payments are not considered expenses, but they do require cash outflows.

The **Current Ratio** is taking your current assets and dividing them by your current liabilities. Your current assets are everything that your business owns that is of value and that you expect to use or convert to cash within a year or the normal operating cycle. Examples of current assets include your cash in the bank, inventory, accounts receivable, etc. Your current liabilities are those obligations of the business that you expect to pay within a year. Current liabilities usually consist of accounts payable, unearned revenues, credit cards, and short-term notes payable. You can find your current assets and current liability data on your **Balance Sheet**.

Calculating your **Current Ratio** helps you to analyze your liquidity and to see if you'll have enough liquid assets to be able to pay your current obligations. A word of caution, this doesn't cover your normal operating expenses, only your liabilities. So if your current assets equal $2,000 and your current liabilities equal $1,000, then your current ratio is 2:1. This means that for every dollar of current liability, you have two dollars of current assets to cover it. A **Current Ratio** of less than 1:1 means that you are not able to cover your current liabilities unless you sell more or acquire additional cash in some way.

Return on Assets ratio helps you to analyze how wisely you are utilizing your assets to generate net income. The only reason we spend money is to make money. Through analysis of how much net income you are generating on your assets, you can see whether you are earning a high or low return on the investment of those assets. Look at it this way, if your net income equals $1,000 and your average total assets equal $10,000, then your **Return on Assets** would be calculated by taking $1,000 divided by $10,000. This equates to 10%.

This means that for every $1 of assets you have, you are earning a return of 10 cents of net income. A higher **Return on Assets** ratio is desired. We want to be making wise decisions in the purchase of our assets to ensure that we are using them in the revenue-generating process. Total assets include cash in the bank, inventory, property, plant, equipment, vehicles, etc. To get your total average assets, you add the beginning plus the ending values for total assets and divide by two.

The **Debt Ratio** provides you the breakdown of how you are financing your assets. You purchase assets and finance them through debt or equity. Outside lenders watch this ratio very closely because the higher your debt, the more your risk increases. If your debt ratio is 40%, then 40% of your assets are financed through outside parties (lenders). This means that 60% of your assets are financed internally through equity.

Comparative analysis with prior periods and industry standards allows you to analyze how you are doing with all of the previous ratios for a period of time. But remember, one ratio doesn't provide much benefit. You should be calculating the ratios and comparing those numbers to your competitors and prior periods. Some factors should include your industry, your length of time in business and general economic environmental influences to determine what target ratios are for each of the listed ratios for your business.

Each business is different so there is no magical number. This is where having a Management

35

Accountant that is experienced in this analysis can help you understand even more about the ratio analysis of your business.

Cole was feeling relief after attending this seminar because he felt better prepared to move into the position of taking over the company from his dad. It was important to him that the business continues to be successful and that he becomes the best owner that he could. Cole knew there would be times that he might have questions, but he at least knew the terminology and could ask questions of his accountant to ensure that he was being proactive in the management of the business.

NOTES

NOTES

CRISTI

Cristi is in her mid-thirties and has been in business for about four years in Missouri. Her promotional advertisement business has been steadily increasing and she's looking to move it out of her basement and into a storefront on the main street in her town. She believes that her business has been profitable enough to warrant the move. Cristi feels strongly that the move is destined to take her business to the next level, which will mean even more profit! She knows there will be some added costs, but Cristi has no doubt that she'll be able to cover those costs with the increased sales that a storefront will bring her. She knows of competitors who have tried this and were not successful. However, Cristi is confident that they didn't have her level of business skills or sales and that's why they failed. What kind of analysis needs to be considered prior to this move?

The first step in getting the storefront is preparing financial statements for her banker. It's going to take

39

some money to remodel the storefront and so she's requested a loan from her bank to help her cover those upfront improvement costs. In order to get the process started, the bank needs her financial statements prior to reviewing her loan application.

Financial Statements? Cristi wasn't sure what her banker wants as she's never had a business loan before and never created financial statements for herself...why would she? She knew she was making money and she didn't have time to do that kind of stuff with everything else that was going on in her life.

The three basic financial statements that you want to create for both forecasting and for determining actual numbers are:

1. Profit/Loss Statement
2. Balance Sheet
3. Cash Flow Statement

Each of these provides a very different view of your business and it is imperative that you have the combination of these to review.

The **Profit/Loss Statement** provides information on Sales (aka Revenues) and Expenses for a period of time. Activities bringing money into the business through the sale of products or services are classified as sales. The money that we expend to generate sales are classified as expenses. We will have direct expenses that are classified as Cost of Goods Sold and indirect expenses that are classified as Administrative & Operating (A&O) Expenses. The net result of **Sales – Cost of Goods Sold = Gross Profit – A&O Expenses = Net Profit/Loss.** We prepare a Profit/Loss Statement for a period of time, which is usually monthly, quarterly, or annually.

The **Balance Sheet** provides a snap shot of the balances in the Assets, Liability and Equity accounts as of a specific statement date. Assets are items the business owns that are of value and include such categories as Cash, Accounts Receivable, Inventory,

Prepaid Expenses, Investments, Property, Plant and Equipment, etc. Liabilities are obligations of the business and include such categories as Accounts Payable, Notes Payable, Credit Card Payables, and Unearned Revenues. Equity is the residual between Assets and Liabilities and represents the claims of the owners on the assets. **The Balance Sheet Equation is: ASSETS= LIABILITIES + EQUITY.**

The **Cash Flow Statement** outlines the activities bringing cash into the business and taking cash out of the business for a period of time. Having a breakdown of those activities provides a clearer financial picture. The three categories on a Cash Flow Statement are: Operating, Investing and Financing. The Operating section covers the daily activities. The Investing section outlines the long-term asset activities. The Financing section shows the changes in cash from the owner and from third-party financing activities. Or you can simply do a breakdown of **Beginning Cash+Cash Inflows-Cash Outflows=Ending Cash.** Either way, you will be able to see exactly where the money is coming in and going out.

Financial statements allow us to take the daily transactional process and transform the numbers into a format that we can use to communicate information about our business, both internally and externally. Knowing just the bottom line of how much profit you have has limited benefit. The full value comes from doing the analysis and understanding how these financial statements can provide better insight into your company's performance.

You don't have to be the world's greatest financial analyst to do these simple calculations. The key is knowing the format and what the results mean. You can calculate some fundamental ratios and gain a new view of your business. You might think that a bunch of numbers won't add value to your business, but you'll be surprised once you start analyzing. If you have the numbers in an easy to understand format, such as in a financial statement, and know how to read them, then you will have limitless angles to assess the strengths and weaknesses of your business.

NOTES

NOTES

DAWN AND CODY

Dawn and her husband Cody are in their late 50's and own an orchard and pumpkin farm in Western Iowa. This is their second season. While their community is very supportive of their idea in thought, many of those same supporters don't want to have to 'pay' to visit their orchard and pumpkin farm. The community has been very verbal in that they shouldn't charge admission. But what those visitors don't understand is how much it takes to run the orchard and pumpkin farm.

There are a lot of costs such as insurance, taxes, contract labor, seeds, equipment, employees, fertilizer, activity supplies, and the list goes on and on. Yet how do Cody and Dawn help the public understand that they are getting a great value for their low admission fee? Or are they charging more than the market can handle?

Dawn and Cody are determined to make this business a success because it is a perfect fit for their retirement plans and their community's needs. It affords them the kind of income they want to be able to enjoy life and travel during their "off" season. They know the idea is good and that they don't have any local competition within a 90-mile radius. However, being from a small community, they are finding that people sure want everything for free! Where else can families enjoy a full day of family entertainment for less than $20? Have you been to the movies lately? You cannot get your family into the movies with treats for that price...let alone a wholesome day of fun on the farm enjoying hayrides, pumpkin carving, picking fruit, feeding the animals, riding the old-fashioned trikes and more!

Dawn has already done the analysis on their business to know that their pricing is right where it needs to be for them to Break-even and attain the profit goals that they have set for their business. They have two accountants that are part of their management team: one focuses on taxes and the other focuses on Management Accounting. Both aspects are critical to their success and she is so thankful that her friend,

Irene, suggested that she have both of the accountants on her team.

Dawn and Cody meet with their Management Accountant monthly and their Tax Accountant quarterly to ensure that their business stays on track. They know it is important to have someone who is knowledgeable in those areas to keep them accountable.

Each month their Management Accountant reviews their bookkeeping and prepares financial statements, which includes a Balance Sheet, Profit/Loss Statement, and a Cash Flow Statement. They also review a series of ratios that include a Return on Assets, a Current Ratio, a Gross Profit Margin Ratio, and a Net Profit Margin Ratio each month. They compare the ratios to the previous period and year for their business and the industry average. This helps them to see that they are gradually improving the overall performance of their business.

Dawn and Cody have seen many of their friends fail in businesses and they don't want to make those same mistakes. They want to enjoy their retirement instead of having to work full-time the rest of their lives.

Dawn and Cody's main focus now is to show the value added services that their farm provides to the local community. Dawn has been working with the local schools, community organizations, and Chamber of Commerce to promote their farm because she realizes it is all about marketing and creating that valued relationship so that people don't see their business as a cost. Instead customers should view it as a great way to spend the day with their family doing outdoor activities and just having plain old-fashioned fun! Dawn is sure that with their focus on providing a solid financial foundation and her continued community involvement, their business will continue to flourish.

It's a fine balance, but Cody and Dawn are confident that their pricing structure based on the Break-even model is ideal. Their goal is to stay strong and show the value they add to the community. Decreasing their prices may put them out of business. If they drop their price a dollar or more, they will not be able to make up that lost revenue due to the fact that the number of potential visitors will not offset that decrease in admission. And then where would they be? They know they can't fall prey to a few complaints, as you can't please everyone. Strong business planning will help them succeed!

NOTES

PATTY AND JAN

Patty and Jan have been best friends for twenty years and both live in Northern Illinois. Patty's background is in Marketing and Jan's is in Computer Technology. They decided to strike out on their own last year by providing marketing services to businesses within their local community. Neither of them have a strong financial background so they know they need someone to help them. Patty is focused on finding someone who specializes in taxes because she doesn't want to pay any more money to "Uncle Sam" then she needs to. Jan thinks they should have someone to help them with their business Management Accounting. What questions should they be asking themselves each month so make sure they have everything in order so that their business is a success?

Some people think that one accountant will be sufficient when it comes to understanding the 'numbers part' of running a business. Is one doctor sufficient to care for all parts of our bodies? Do you have just one doctor? Most of us have doctors for different parts of our body. It's the same concept for our business because our business has many different aspects. While we may not be able to afford to have a full-time staff that specializes in all of those areas, it is relatively easy to find specialists who provide consulting for small businesses. So instead of finding one who is a jack-of-all-trades, it can benefit our business by having input from a variety of specialists; which will help us see our business from different views and make sure that no one "ailment" causes the demise of our business. The key is ensuring that your team of professionals will all work together for the best outcome for the overall business.

Both Patty and Jan are correct. They need to have someone who can help them understand the myriad of tax issues that their business encounters. That individual may or may not be able to provide insight on the management aspects. Each accountant has different specialties and Patty and Jan need to ensure that they find the right mixture of those specialties that blend well with their individual business needs.

Remember though, there is a difference between hiring a Bookkeeper and an Accountant. An Accountant is a professional who is able to provide analysis of your financials for you and help you understand how to utilize that information in business, whereas a Bookkeeper's skills may be limited to strictly the input of data and the basics of record keeping. It's like any profession, make sure you do your due diligence to ensure that whoever you hire is a good fit for your needs. There's not one credential that guarantees you ultimate success.

Some of the designations/certifications that you may see in the Accounting and Bookkeeping professions include Certified Management Accountant, Certified Financial Manager, Enrolled Agent, Certified Bookkeeper, Certified Payroll Specialist, Certified Public Accountant, Tax Preparer and others. Don't just take these designations/certifications at face value. You still need to be sure that they have the right knowledge and experience that is a fit for your company.

Patty and Jan decided that having two financial professionals would provide them the broadest base of knowledge. They knew it would be important to make sure everyone was a team player so that they were not being counter-productive. Patty and Jan interviewed dozens of accountants and were able to find two that specialized in small businesses. Their Tax Specialist, Melissa, helped them to understand the differences in business formation and how that would affect their taxes. Melissa also reviewed with them the various ways they could take profits out of their businesses based upon the various legal formations.

There are also different ways in which you can structure the acquisition of the assets that you need in your business including purchasing and leasing. Different tax reasons make each of these desirable to different businesses and you need to have that advice prior to acquisition. Working with a Tax Specialist on an ongoing basis provides you reassurance that you are making wise tax decisions throughout the year. Waiting until April of the following year has limited opportunities for you to go back and redo anything for the prior year.

If you work with a Tax Specialist on an ongoing basis, you are able to proactively make those decisions so that they benefit your business in the best possible way. There are other types of taxes you may need to address in your business such as property taxes, sales and use taxes, employment taxes and more. Don't mess around with tax issues. Start your business on the right foot and get advice from the start so that you don't have to have any regrets after the fact. The penalties and interest assessments from the various levels of government have put many businesses out of business, and I am sure that you don't want to be one of those statistics!

Patty and Jan found Monica who had years of accounting and entrepreneurial experience. She was down to earth and never made Patty or Jan feel inadequate about the running of their business. Monica partnered with them on a monthly basis to review their bookkeeping and ensure that their monthly financial statements accurately portrayed the picture of their business. The financial statements Monica prepared consisted of a Cash Flow Statement, a Balance Sheet, and a Profit/Loss Statement. She also helped them perform some basic financial ratios to ensure that their business was on track and was growing steadily. Those ratios included the Current Ratio, Debt Ratio, Gross Profit Margin Ratio, Net Profit Margin Ratio, Return on Assets, and others.

Monica was truly a blessing for Patty and Jan! She was easily accessible by phone or email throughout the month any time they had questions, so it felt like they had their own CFO (Chief Financial Officer) on staff, but they sure enjoyed not having the burden of paying her a full-time salary!

Patty and Jan would never have guessed two years ago that they would be as financially comfortable with their business as they are today. They know they don't know all the answers, however, they have a great team of consultants to compliment their skills and ensure the continued success of their business. Patty and Jan's strong business management was what won them the local "Best Small Business" award this year through their local Chamber of Commerce. Who would have thought they would win that award?

NOTES

DONNA

Donna's in her late 60's and just retired from her position as a hospital administrator after 40 years with the same company. Donna is starting a consulting company in Colorado to help small physician offices and hospitals with temporary administrator services on a 'PRN' or 'as-needed' basis. She thoroughly enjoyed her career and didn't want to give it up altogether, but she did want more flexibility to spend time with her husband and family.

Donna needs someone to help her with some of the basic administrative issues and wondered what the best option would be for her. Should she contract with a temporary agency or what should she so? She called her friend Sally to see what she did for her office help. Sally explained that there were a number of factors Donna would need to consider before she made any commitments. Some of the questions Donna would need to think about included:

- How many hours would they work daily/weekly?
- How consistent would the hours be week to week?
- What type of work responsibilities would they have?
- Are there any special skills needed?
- Where would the individual work? Onsite at her office or at his/her own home?
- What amount of money did she have budgeted for her assistant?

Sally explained that there are advantages and disadvantages with all options. When you are hiring an employee, you not only need to focus on the actual pay rate, but you also have to consider the extra insurance, taxes, benefits, record keeping, and incidental costs that you will incur with an employee. It may not sound like a lot, but it can be substantial. It is wise to assess your various options to see what the best fit is for your individual business.

Committing to employees is a step that should not be taken lightly. Most business owners will need to strengthen their presence in the market through additional people. However, the structuring of those relationships and the work those individuals will be performing can make the difference between a positive or negative impact on your bottom line.

After careful review of the pros and cons of her analysis, Donna determined that utilizing subcontractors to do the administrative duties would be the best fit for her business. This would enable her to utilize the services when she needed them and not incur any unnecessary overhead costs. As her business grows, she can reassess her needs and determine what the right course of action would be.

NOTES

KATE

Kate is in her mid-forties and decided six months ago that her corporate career was no longer a fit for her. She decided it was time to join the ranks of small business owners in her local community in Western Kansas even though she was a little nervous about this midlife change. Her business was a small craft store where she sublet space to multiple craft producers. She'd seen these stores when she visited her daughter on the East Coast and thought it was a great idea.

Part of her contract with these smaller producers was that Kate would provide a one-stop shop for the customer to get a variety of gift purchases and Kate would provide the advertising for them as a group. Kate had done some research on various types of advertising and was finding that it was quite expensive; in fact, the costs were more than she had originally anticipated. But how could she find a way to bring people in the door without spending all of her profits on advertising?

Kate joined a local women's roundtable group so that she could enhance her business knowledge. Though she had spent many years in business as a banker and manager, she had a learning curve on how to apply those skills to her new position of 'business owner'. She was learning from her roundtable meetings about the various aspects of entrepreneurship and felt it was going to make a big impact to the success of her business. Each month, a different entrepreneur got to have her day in the 'Hot Seat', and when it was time for Kate to speak to the group, she presented her biggest challenges and the other women focused on helping her with creative solutions.

After returning from her roundtable meeting, Kate had a page and a half of ideas that she thought were very viable and fit well with her marketing plan. She realized she couldn't continue to use costly advertising options, but instead she needed to focus on how she was spending her time doing the marketing for the business. Her associates at the roundtable meeting suggested she start networking more due to the fact that it had lower costs and higher returns. Plus, each of the women had stories to share about their other networking groups and outcomes they had seen in their businesses.

Cindy, Kate's accountant, was coming the next day to work on the budget for next year. Kate would be visiting with Cindy about cutting back on her advertising budget so that she could raise her profit margin. Another idea given to her at the roundtable was that she should be measuring the return on her investment for the advertising she did. The group suggested various ways to do the measuring so that Kate could track where her customers were hearing about her store. This information would help Kate to know where to focus her time and money for marketing. Kate knew Cindy would be able to assist her with the details of this process.

Kate was pleased that she had several opportunities to have people mentoring her through this process. Running a small business can be very overwhelming, even for a seasoned individual. She knew there was no reason for her to stress over 'wearing too many hats' because she had surrounded herself with an attorney, an accountant, her roundtable-mentoring group, great employees and a myriad of other entrepreneurs! Things would get easier and Kate was determined to make it a successful venture.

NOTES

NOTES

STACI

Staci is the owner of a new salon in Southern Missouri. Staci is 29 and has been in the industry for the last ten years. While she knows it is a risk, she also believes that the only way she can achieve her goals is to be her own boss. She was able to receive an SBA (Small Business Administration) backed-loan and although the last year has been full of ups and downs, she just announced her grand opening last month!

She is located in a busy strip mall in the community of 60,000 and is excited and nervous about what the future holds for her. She developed a business plan when she was in the planning phase of her business. Things have changed slightly from her original plans and she needs to finalize her budget for the upcoming year.

She is a little unsure of the budgeting process since her sales are difficult to project, but she also knows she has to have some kind of target for her business. She's got a large rent and loan payment to make she covers each month, plus all the operating expenses. Oh yeah…then there's profit too. She went into business for herself so that she could make more money as the boss than she could as an employee. Why is a budget important?

Staci is working with her accountant on preparing a budget. One of the easiest templates to work with is the format of your Profit/Loss Statement. All that needs to be done is to add an additional part at the bottom for extra cash inflows/outflows that aren't classified as revenues or expenses. The benefit of using a similar layout is that it makes it easier to understand 'actual' compared to 'budgeted' analysis throughout the year.

If you don't spend time at the end of each period (month, quarter, or year) analyzing what actually happened in your business compared to what you anticipated happening, then there is no reason to do a budget. Some accounting packages have budget features in the software to assist you. Some also provide preformatted reports to make it easy for you to analyze the differences between actual and budgeted figures.

If you don't prepare a budget, then how do you know where you are going? A budget is a roadmap for your business. For example, if you want to achieve a $100,000 net cash inflow next year, how are you going to get there? Are you going to plan for the future or just wait and see what happens? Failing to plan is a plan for failure.

By utilizing a budget, you can break the financial picture down into small steps of a month and consider what revenues, expenses, and additional cash inflows/outflows you will have each month to get you to that overall goal. It's too overwhelming to start by looking at the big goal. By breaking your goals into manageable pieces, you'll be able to focus on the small steps that will lead you to the achievement of your larger goal.

NOTES

CONCLUSION

Can you see yourself in any or all of these situations? If so, you are not alone! Just because you are a small business owner, it doesn't mean that you can't have a team. The benefit is that you surround yourself with those who will assist you in reaching your goals! Failure is sure to fall upon those that think they have to be all things to their business. Why add that much stress to your world?

You are in business to enjoy what you do, so stop stressing! Find someone to be on your team to help you take control of your business. There's no better time like the present to change the path your business is on. Or perhaps you've been in the 'red' and you have already utilized some of these concepts to move your business into the 'black'! All of the stories in this book have shown us that nothing can help a business more than information…it's what we all need to ensure our businesses run to their full potential.

All of these concepts can take your business from a state of barely surviving to one where you can enjoy being a business owner. We often laugh when people say running a business is 'easy'. I believe it is only those who have never done it that would classify being an entrepreneur as 'easy'. Though it doesn't have to be a life of late nights where we are fretting over why we can't pay our bills. Life is too short to not enjoy it. So keep this book as a tool to help you.

Do you know the answers to the checklist provided at the end of this section? If not, challenge yourself to find the answers. Ignoring reality doesn't change it...if your business is not doing well; it's not going to get better without effort from you. So be objective when you look at your business and see where you can enhance it. Implement these concepts to keep your business 'out of the red'! You'll be thankful you did when you can reap the benefits of entrepreneurism!

I hope that you have benefited from the stories that were shared throughout the book as much as I did from those entrepreneurs that have touched my life through my consulting business. We are given so many great opportunities in our lives...it's up to us whether or not we seize those opportunities!

Congratulations to you on being dedicated enough to your business to allocate the time to read this book, but don't stop now. Take these concepts and implement them into your business with the help of your Management Accountant and you'll be amazed at where you're business will go!

Do you have a story you'd like to share? Please feel free to email them to pam@rppc.net.

I believe passion allows people to change their dreams into reality so '**Wish it...Dream it...Do it**'!

DO YOU KNOW:

- [ ] How to prepare a Cash Flow Statement?
- [ ] How to prepare a Profit/Loss Statement?
- [ ] How to prepare a Balance Sheet?
- [ ] How to calculate your Gross Profit Margin Ratio?
- [ ] How to calculate your Net Profit Margin Ratio?
- [ ] How to calculate your Debt Ratio?
- [ ] How to calculate your Return on Assets Ratio?
- [ ] How to calculate your Current Ratio?
- [ ] How to calculate your Break-even Point?
- [ ] How to analyze the 'full cost' of employees?

If your answer to any of these is "NO", challenge yourself to find it out...your business will thank you!

TERMS AND DEFINITIONS

Accounts Payable – Liability created by buying goods or services on credit. It is also the amount you owe a vendor on account.

Accounting – Information and measurement system that identifies, records and communicates relevant information about a company's business activities.

Accounting Equation – Assets = Liabilities + Equity

Accounts Receivable – Amounts due from customers for credit sales. It is also when you've completed the work and they haven't paid you.

Assets – Resources a business owns or controls that are expected to provide current and future benefits to the business. Examples include cash, accounts receivable, inventory, property, plants, and equipment.

Balance Sheet – Financial statement that lists assets, liabilities and equity balances as of a specific date.

Bookkeeping – Part of accounting that involves recording transactions and events in dollars and cents.

Break-even Point – Point at which a businesses' revenues and expenses are equal.

Budget – Process of projecting future sales and expenses (i.e. Profit/Loss Budget). It can also incorporate non-sale and non-expense related cash items depending on the format of the budget (i.e. Cash Flow Budget).

Cash Flow Statement – Financial statement showing the changes in cash for a specific period of time.

Contribution Margin – Equals sales minus variable costs that are utilized in computing your Break-even point.

Contribution Margin Ratio – Contribution margin in dollars divided by sales dollars.

Cost of Goods Sold – Direct costs of sales including materials and labor.

Current Assets – Cash and other assets expected to be sold, collected, or used within one year or the company's operating cycle, whichever is longer.

Current Liabilities – Obligations due to be paid back within a year or the operating cycle, whichever is longer.

Current Ratio – Ratio used to evaluate a company's ability to pay its short-term obligations. Ratio is calculated by dividing current assets by current liabilities.

Debt Ratio – Ratio of total liabilities to total assets, which is used to reflect risk, associated with a company's debts.

Direct Expenses – Expenses that are a direct part of the goods that you are selling. Includes direct materials and direct labor. See Cost of Goods Sold.

Equity – Owner's claim on the assets of a business. It also equals the residual interest in an entity's assets after deducting liabilities.

Fixed Expenses – Expenses that do not fluctuate in relationship with business activities.

Gross Profit Margin Ratio – Gross profit margin (sales minus cost of goods sold) divided by net sales.

Indirect Expenses – Amounts spent to generate revenues but they are not a direct part of the goods you produce. Examples include rent, taxes, advertising, administrative salaries, interest, etc.

Liabilities – Creditors' claims on an organization's assets; involves a probable future payment of assets, products, or services that a company is obligated to make due to past transactions or events.

Management Accounting – Area of accounting mainly aimed at serving the decision-making needs of internal users.

Net Income – Amount earned after subtracting all expenses necessary for and matched with sales for a period. Also called income, net profit, or earnings.

Net Profit Margin Ratio – Ratio of a company's net income to its net sales. It is also known as the percent of income in each dollar of revenue.

Profit/Loss Statement – Financial statement that subtracts expenses from revenues to yield a net income or loss over a specified period of time. Also called an Income Statement.

Return on Assets – Measure of a company's ability to use its assets to generate net income, which is computed by dividing net income by average total assets.

Revenues – Selling of products or services within a business. Also called sales.

Variable expenses – Expenses that fluctuate in direct relationship with business activities.

SEMINARS

Some of the seminars offered by the author include topics such as:

Accounting ABC's

Alleviating 'Go-For' Delegation

Basics of Bookkeeping

Break-Even Analysis

Business Plan Basics

Entrepreneurship

Financial Statement Fundamentals

Making Sense of Financial Ratios

Networking Fundamentals

And more...

For more information, visit our website at www.rppc.net.

ABOUT THE AUTHOR

Pam Newman, President of RPPC, Inc., has a diverse background with extensive experience in businesses ranging from entrepreneurial start-ups to Fortune 500 organizations; which include academic, banking, construction, restaurant, telecommunication, and training industries. Pam's passion is helping entrepreneurs by Realizing Profitable Potential through Change. RPPC, Inc., which is a woman-owned and operated business enterprise.

Pam's focus is helping entrepreneurs succeed in their business through small business training and consulting services. Please visit RPPC Inc.'s website for more information at www.rppc.net. All services are customized to meet the individual client's needs. Pam has a strong belief in the educational aspects of her services and has built the foundation of her company on providing training and consulting services with the client's involvement. This method establishes a solid foundation for her clients as they grow their businesses.

If you can see that these concepts are important in your business and you'd like to attend one of Pam's trainings or schedule individual consulting, please e-mail her at pam@rppc.net.